I0118822

James Fotheringham

Wordsworth's Prelude

As a Study of Education

James Fotheringham

Wordsworth's Prelude
As a Study of Education

ISBN/EAN: 9783337218454

Printed in Europe, USA, Canada, Australia, Japan

Cover: Foto ©Thomas Meinert / pixelio.de

More available books at **www.hansebooks.com**

WORDSWORTH'S "PRELUDE"

AS A

STUDY OF EDUCATION

BY

JAMES FOTHERINGHAM

AUTHOR OF

"STUDIES OF THE MIND AND ART OF ROBERT BROWNING"

LONDON

HORACE MARSHALL & SON

TEMPLE HOUSE, TEMPLE

AVENUE, E.C

1899

NOTE

Parts of this Essay were originally read to the Bradford Branch of the Teachers' Guild. Their wish to have it is one reason for its publication. But as now issued it is much fuller than and otherwise different from the paper they heard with such friendly interest.

J. F.

August, 1899.

WORDSWORTH'S *PRELUDE*
AS A
STUDY OF EDUCATION

THE *Prelude* has suffered the usual fate of long poems, especially when such poems are of a philosophical cast, of an intellectual texture—it has been but little read even by readers of the other poetry of its author—his lyrics and odes. And yet it has some of Wordsworth's most characteristic poetry, and not a little of his characteristic wisdom. Few, indeed, of the poet's works are more important for the comprehension of his Ethic than this "philosophic Song of Truth which cherishes our daily life" (*Prelude*, i. 229–30).

But this poem was not published by its author, nor was it named by him. It was published by the poet's wife shortly after his death, and its title was assigned by her. As to both points she showed that insight and judgment which made her through so many years a true helpmeet of the poet in the things of his genius as of his life. It must have been touching for her just then to give the public this record of years so long gone past.

And the *Prelude*, in fact, belongs to an early time in the work of the poet. It was deliberately composed at intervals during a period of some six years—the years following the poet's settlement at Grasmere. The "preamble" of the poem (cf. bk. vii. 1-12) was made at the time when, on leaving Goslar, the poet felt the "quickening breeze" that met him as he turned his face again to his own country. This stir of feeling and thought led him to sing "with fervour irresistible" the theme that came to him as he reviewed his past and considered his future. That fervid impulse was "short-lived," but the theme was soon resumed with "less impetuous stream," that flowed steadily for a time and then stopped for some years. It was again taken up in "the primrose time" five years later, and finished after a further interval in the following year.

The poem was thus composed between February, 1799, and May, 1805. About half of it had been composed by the end of April, 1804; a great part of the rest of it

was done between October and December
of 1804; and the closing books during April
and May, 1805, after the death of the poet's
brother, John Wordsworth.

It was dedicated to the friend on whose
interest and sympathy he could implicitly
count—Samuel Taylor Coleridge. Coleridge took five books of it with him when
he went to Malta in 1804, and the whole
poem was read to him in December, 1806.
It was revised in 1832; but the poet left
it unpublished for more than forty years.
Coleridge was greatly impressed by its
verse and its matter, by its poetry and its
truth. He speaks of it (vide *Sibylline Leaves*,
"To William Wordsworth") as

> An Orphic song indeed,
> A song divine of high and passionate thoughts,
> To their own music chaunted!

But, in the judgment of its author, the time
had not come for its publication, and that
time did not arrive during his own life.
The *Prelude* is, in fact, in the nature of an
autobiography, and an autobiography of a
special kind. The sub-title of the poem
gives the kind and its theme. It is, so the
title justly tells us, the story of *The Growth
of a Poet's Mind*. Coleridge's phrase had
been "the growth of an individual mind"—

the story of "the foundations and growth of
a human spirit." Now the study of a poet's
life, uneventful as such lives mostly are,
might seem bad enough; but the history of
a poet's mind—the unfolding of his genius,
of his poetic intuition and principles, what
is called with a shrug a " psychological
study," a study of moral growth and little
more—seems to be many degrees worse.
Wordsworth possibly felt this, and partly
deferred to it. But besides this, he felt that
his own position in English poetry, and the
interest so far shown in his work, scarcely
justified such length and intimacy of autobiography as the *Prelude* contained, although
indeed his poetic position was fairly recognised in the late "thirties," and his value
well assured some years before his death.

The recognition of the poem after its
issue in the summer of 1850 was cold
enough. It was the " Life," we may say,
of the most original poet of his time. It
threw a flood of light on his mental history
and growth during the most important
period of that history and growth, and
through his experience and course of
thought it cast much light on the life of
his time during important years of that age
of revolutions. But the public had other

interests, and did not see the interest or the significance of these things.

A few things have, however, happened since 1850, and not the least of them, perhaps, a considerable intellectual and spiritual change. The world seems to move in the line of growth of its greater and more original poets ; and works which one generation finds obscure, impossible, the next finds legible and quick with meaning. The *Prelude* may seem a case in point. We have now a pocket edition of the poem, and a considerable and excellent volume by a French scholar devoted to its study.

The poem, we have said, is an "Autobiography"—that delicate and dangerous, and yet in the best instances how interesting, kind of autobiography which is termed "spiritual autobiography"—a history not of events or doings, but of thoughts, feelings, experiences and vital constructions. In such writings it is hard rather to see the facts that are to be presented, to see them with clear eyes and in due proportions, to know what is valuable and what is not, to keep out the distortions of egoism, the taint of morbidity. It is desirable to escape these defects, these faults, and not easy to do so in this kind of writings; so we say. And

yet it has to be admitted that there are
autobiographies which by no means fulfil
these conditions, and still are most interesting, and are so, moreover, in part because
they do not fulfil the above conditions of
" good autobiography." The age of Wordsworth, as we all know, saw an astonishing
instance of this in the *Confessions* of Rousseau, that document of "the age of feeling."

The work before us is, anyhow, a sound
and healthy record. It was done, we have
seen, in the poet's best years. Its best passages stand safely among the best parts of
his work. It throws much light on the
larger principles of his interpretation of
nature and human nature. Its grasp of his
poetic ideas is firm, its statement of them
fresh and luminous. It may be that the
poem is too long for its theme, that it is
tiresome in parts, and heavy at times. Its
temper and diction are too uniformly weighty
and serious ; but it is honest and lofty and
true. Distinctly self-conscious it may be—
that is in the point of view, and in the process of the work—but it is proudly sincere,
and, in spite of the risks of its theme, it is
surely free from vanity. As Mr. F. Myers
has said, "You can read it with implicit

confidence." And, as M. Legouis says, "There are no theatrical attitudes," no arrangements or utterances for effect. The poet knows his own value too well for that kind of show. He has "too much pride to be vain." His aim, let us say, was simply to trace his own growth, to know his own powers, his principles, himself, the gifts and truths his culture had brought him and the destiny of his mind. His aim was no way to determine the "merit" of those powers and attainments. He does not think of their value in relation to others.

It will now be clear that the *Prelude* may be usefully and suggestively studied on several sides—literary, historical, ethical. It may, of course, be taken in the literary and historical way, and considered fruitfully with reference to its sources in the life and literature of the time. Professor Legouis has done very good work here. It may be taken as a study of the "origin and progress" of this poet's powers—the rise and growth within his experience of his gifts and insights. It may be regarded in a more general way as a study of man—of man as this poet knew him, in relation to man's whole environment in nature and human nature. Or it may be regarded in relation

to the poet's works as "the prelude" to
those, setting forth in a deliberate and
deeply-considered introduction the grounds
and elements of that interpretation of nature
and human nature which the rest of his
works were to illustrate and unfold. It was
in this light and relation that Mrs. Wordsworth took the poem when she called it the
Prelude. For her it was the first great
section of his total work. It was for her an
"Essay" opening his work as a whole,
giving for the years up to his maturity as
man and poet his experience, his discipline,
his point of view, the factors and attainments of his culture, his fundamental principles as a poet and master of life.

It will be seen from the title of this essay
which of the lines thus sketched has been
selected for consideration now. It is the
Prelude as a study of education simply
we propose to take on this occasion. Our
specific aim is to show the value and interest
of the *Prelude* in this aspect of it, to set
out the principles and truths of this poetry,
the ideas and intuitions of this poet, in their
bearing on education in its larger sense and
scope. This seemed an inquiry very suitable for a guild of teachers, and not less
suitable because somewhat off the usual

track of professional discussions regarding education.

Students of the *Prelude*, whether they regard its literary or its biographic value, may indeed raise objections. They may urge that the poet conceived and planned the poem as a study of the poetic mind— of his own mind—and that, in the phrase of Coleridge, a highly " individual mind," with a unique experience. But allowing its full value to this view of such work, it cannot be thought that that is its whole value, or even the better part of its value. For the poet as poet is not apart from other men, however much he may for a time be ahead of them. He is, we may say, in virtue of his powers, a leader and helper of other men, a bringer of joy to them out of the deeper, fresher wells of his nature and experience. Other men are his heirs, and in time enter into his experiences. If his experience were not in measure yet sincerely open to other men, then Art were an illusion or an impossibility. Its appeal to us, and our sympathy with it, spring from kinship in nature and community of experience. The poet, with reference to his own matters, is quicker, more vital, richer it may be, than most of us, but the principles and the laws are the same for all of us, and the last test of the poet's vision and genius is his power to bring other men to see what he has seen, to enjoy what has pleased him, to be what he is in the things where he is most human.

The general plan of the *Prelude* is to follow the course of the poet's life, and select the things and the events in its course which had a significant influence in shaping his mind and his character, in unfolding his intellectual powers and principles, and the moral elements of his nature as well. And the survey of things and events from this point of view is full of meaning. In its mere conception, in its starting-point, in what it selects and in what it omits, there was much significance at a time when the whole question of education was under discussion and when treatises on the subject were a fashion, and many new and plausible schemes of human culture were being zealously advocated as a part of the passion of the time for human improvement.

And our poet's survey, if the *Prelude* be taken as in a certain true sense a "treatise" on education, was, we say, extremely significant in its conception of culture, in its starting-point, and in the things put forth as really influential. In the large conception of the poem regarded from the educational point of view there was great significance, since it presented " the growth of a mind " from childhood to maturity, and yet took all that was merely scholastic, technical, formal, as incidental rather than essential—as even relatively unimportant. It may be thought that this was in the theme, and in the poet's purpose as a poet, and, of course, there is truth there ; otherwise the *Prelude* would not have been a poem, though it might have been a " treatise " of much interest. Yet that surely in no way lessens the significance of the conception from our present point of view, seeing that it is of the very substance of the conception that, as regards both intellectual and moral growth, life is a scheme of stimulus, discipline, training, in which the scholastic and academic elements and factors are always subsidiary and often comparatively unimportant. Hawkshead Grammar School did not badly for William Wordsworth. It taught him Latin pretty well, and some mathematics, and one teacher there made a distinct and genial impression on the boy. And St. John's College, Cambridge, according to the temper of the age and its " lights," and as far as he let it, may be said to have

done fairly for the by no means studious
north country youth entrusted to her care.
But in the scheme of his true culture as he
saw and described it in his early manhood,
when the scheme had become clear to
him, neither St. John's College nor the old
Grammar School counted for much with reference to that development of his genuine
powers—that self-knowledge and that mas-
tery of himself and of life which were the
basis of all he had thus become and of all
he was to do.

Now from the educationist's point of view
this may appear a heresy or a truism.
Most of us would, when the matter is thus
broadly put, regard it as perfectly " sound
doctrine." We recognise in terms, and as
a general truth, that what is technically
called education is but a part of the real
education of a human being. But, as thus
loosely allowed, the truth has often no
practical value—is, perhaps, only admitted
to be ignored. And the question is, What
is the bearing of the truth so conceived on
the scholastic scheme as such—on its aims,
and on our estimate of the place and scope
of the scheme in life itself? In so far as
the *Prelude* may give clues for a right
answer to that question, it would render an

important service indeed. What clues has it then for an answer to this question which is always facing the educationist, and always bringing his particular scheme and procedure under trenchant criticism? The poet's conception of the mind's growth and of life's real culture, as proceeding through all experience, his idea of life itself as education, is the first point. The *Prelude* makes that stand out as few writings do. We must get a just perception of that. We must clearly and frankly recognise that larger scheme, and in the spirit of Emerson admit that what we do not call education is more precious than that which is so called by us. We must increasingly, and with careful judgment, fit our scholastic means and scheme into the vital order. We can only do this as we are on our guard against what a recent writer has well called the *idola scholarum*, as we keep a free and active sympathy with life, as we see how little our technical means can do as compared with the great things life is always doing.

And then we have said the poet's starting-point is significant. His starting-point is childhood and the child-mind. The interest and importance of childhood and the child-

mind was one of the ruling ideas of Wordsworth's poetry. It was part of the spiritual
movement of the age of Wordsworth, part of
its deeper naturalism. It is well known that
a " return to nature" was, perhaps, the most
characteristic passion and deepest movement in the mind of the later 18th century
in France, England, and Germany, manifest-
ing itself in art and philosophy, in politics
and conduct. Romanticism itself may be
conceived as part of that great movement.
And that "return to nature," to "natural
things and principles," so strongly marked
in the sentiment as in the thought of the
time, led in one aspect of it to what has been
called "the glorification of the savage," and
in another aspect to what has been termed
"the worship of the child." It is clear that
many of those who took up the cry of a
"return to nature"—to work from it, to
reform with it—forgot to inquire what they
meant by nature, though that inquiry was
equally important on the philosophic and
on the practical sides. In the same way it
has to be said that fervid followers of Wordsworth seem apt to forget to ask what their
master really meant by the sovereign importance he gave childhood and the child-
mind in his "scheme of virtues."

Our childhood sits,—
Our simple childhood sits upon a throne
That hath more power than all the elements.
(*Prelude*, v. 508.)

So the poet sings. But in regard to the
culture of life, what does this mean? We
all recognise that mental and moral growth
begin from early childhood, and that a
certain body of principles and habits is unfolded, and partly organized then. That is a
bit of natural history and of interest for the
nursery. But beyond that it would seem
that the doctrine we are considering has
for many no practical use, and is even for
some a piece of misleading sentimentalism.
It was, however, a living principle for the
age of Wordsworth, and one it greatly
needed to break the bonds of the past, to
quicken and enlarge the life of the time.
It has been fruitful in our own century
in many ways, and it is a principle the
educationist surely needs, and tends somewhat to thrust aside.

Let us see, then, by help of the poetry in
which the idea was best interpreted, what
it means, and how it bears on education.
Wordsworth has put it in certain verses
which may be taken as the classical statement of the idea.

> The child is father of the man,
> And I would have my days to be
> Bound each to each by natural piety

—"the child" "father of the man," and "natural piety" as the bond of all our habits and all our days—what law of growth, what truths of culture, do the words contain? The principle is not, perhaps, stated anywhere in the *Prelude* quite so explicitly as in the lines just quoted, but the whole study of growth in that poem is subject to the principle, and throws light on the meaning it had for the poet. At the opening of the poem the poet tells how, in the case of his own mind, impressive training began with the first dawn of childhood. Then, as he came to see his own growth, was "the seed-time of the soul." The voice of the Derwent "blent its murmurs with his nurse's song," and "flowed along his dreams." And all the things of his first days are conceived as bearing a part in the foundation of his powers and the texture of his mind (*Prelude*, bks. i., ii. *passim*). Nor is it a matter of things and experiences only; it is also a matter of affections and principles. The lines above quoted—which are of 1802—set forth a law, enforce a certain loyalty—loyalty to the instincts and principles of childhood; while the lines quoted from the *Prelude* (bk. v.) declare the native strength of the mind, and its power from the first to transform experience—it rules, as we may say, by "right divine."

In such words the poet seems to some of us to speak only as an "oracle" speaks, words of no sure meaning. And, in fact, the words and his doctrine on this matter have been taken often in that way. And yet if we read them in due relation to the movement of which they are a part, they have plain and fruitful meanings. They mean that in all our culture, in our treatment of mind and in our estimates of things, we must respect nature and natural principles. They mean that we must value the great simple things of life and nature, the primitive and general principles and powers of mind and heart. They mean that in one aspect of it the right culture is a loyal evolution of the native powers of the soul, and that we must respect the Ideal implicit in nature, and not seek to constrain her to some idea of ours—to some end arising out of our utilities, our conventions, or our pride. "Natural piety" is thus allegiance to "the nature of things," and to the true order of life. It is fidelity to the great and simple laws of intelligence and morality.

And still to some of us it will seem that we have here only a "counsel of perfection," open to the charge of vague ideality. It goes without saying that only as we do our sensible best to ascertain what in respect of minds the true nature is, and to what principles our obedience is demanded, can any good come of the truth Wordsworth so much emphasized. In part through his own happy experience, and in part through his deep insight into the great movement of which his poetry was so true an expression, Wordsworth at the point in hand grasped one of the greatest principles of the movement to give it his own form. But it often happens that the form into which an original and vivid poetic mind puts a truth partly reveals and in part conceals his principle for many who follow him. It has been so here. Wordsworth's praise of childhood has often been so read that his principle has been missed by mere deference to the " letter " of his statement. And yet the poet had himself put his underlying principle into terse and happy phrases, both in verse and prose. In the preface to the second edition of the *Lyrical Ballads* such statement is found (cf. Works, vi. 308). And there it is ·defined as a " religious " regard for " the essential passions of the heart," for " the primary laws of human nature," for " the sacred simplicities of life." Elsewhere it is seen to be the poet's sense of and reverence for that " empire " which every human being " inherits," and which he stands answerable for "as a natural being in the strength of nature."

It thus appears that Wordsworth's stress on the child-nature, and on other simplicities, was rather a consequence of his principle and spirit than the principle itself from the educational point of view. But, in any case, he did a capital service by his study of a growth and a culture far behind the first schooldays, and behind all teaching through words and notions. It is owing to the movement he so well interpreted, and in good part it is owing to him, that we have studied the child-nature so much and so carefully as we have lately been doing. And, without doubt, all who face the problems and responsibilities of the education of young children, especially now that by law we virtually bring them under a process of formal education so much earlier than we were wont to do—all of us, at least, who are

not, in Professor Laurie's phrase, "teachers
by grace of God," and of the scholastic
tradition as such—will agree that a still
fuller and more exact study of the primary
laws and conditions of intelligence, and of
the factors of mental growth in a well-
ordered educational scheme, is desirable.
We have yet to work out more carefully
the lines on which, the means by which, the
steps through which, the ideas, feelings, and
efforts of children may be healthily and
fruitfully stimulated, guided, unfolded.
Perez, Preyer, Darwin, and Professor Sully
have worked in the field, and they bring
help; but our range of observations is not
as yet sufficiently wide, nor are our generali-
zations on many points sufficiently definite
and exact. And the fallacy of ready inference from single cases, or from a few cases, a
fallacy specially apt to arise in the teacher's
field of practice and observation, has to be
watchfully guarded against, and shut out
from the writings of investigators and from
the judgment and work of teachers.

In other ways also our gains from the
movement and principle we are considering
have been important. It is one of its con-
sequences that more and more our schemes
and machinery in education are being set

to find and to unfold the "nature"—the true powers—of the minds to be trained, and less and less to force "another nature" on them than that which after due care and proper tests we infer to belong to them. The idea of a "nature" in things, which must be observed and respected, is as a working conception comparatively recent. The idea of a "nature" in minds which must be studied and served, not browbeaten, is largely a result of the romantic and scientific movements since the Revolution. It means an attitude of modesty and inquiry towards mind as towards a natural structure, giving up wholly the old notion that you can and may make of minds just what you wish, and in "the best cases" anything whatever. It means that whether there be a "science of mind" practically available for the teacher or not—and some appear to assume a posture of impatience or superiority to extant psychologies—it is the interest and some part of the business of the teacher to study mind in its elements and laws. It is a troublesome study possibly; but once recognise that there is a nature and a "reign of law" in minds, and the inference is straight and swift that the art and matter of teaching must fit themselves to that

nature and its laws, and can do so only
as the teacher understands Mind.

And if Wordsworth's naturalism carries
in it the conception that Mind is a natural
structure and must be so treated, his "natural
piety " carries the conception that the stages
of human growth and culture as they are
bound to each other by vital coherence so
they should be by moral fidelity; and that
only as each stage is honourably treated for
all it is worth, and duly fulfilled, can we
reach integrity and strength, whether of
mind or character. Now this, it will be seen,
is one of Froebel's great ideas; and, in fact,
Froebel and Wordsworth are in frequent
agreement and close sympathy on the matters
of humane education and human welfare.
Froebel was but twelve years younger than
Wordsworth; and though he lived amid
different circumstances and for different
purposes, he belonged to the same natural-
istic and romantic movement, and as the
" prophet and apostle of a kingdom of God "
to be reached through a wise and real education covering the whole of life, his ideas
often, his aims almost always, are such as
the poet of the *Prelude* and the *Excursion*
would have heartily approved. And so
when Froebel, in his mystic way, insists that

human development should go from point to
point, should go steadily, should be viewed
and treated as continuously advancing, when
he insists that the child, the boy, the youth,
the man are not separate from, but intimately
and vitally related to, each other, and that
the vigorous and complete unfolding of each
successive stage of life depends on the
vigour and completeness of the development of the preceding stages (cf. *Student's
Froebel*, Herford, p. 11), Wordsworth would
have understood and heartily agreed. And
when Froebel further insists that while we
must foresee development—must see the man
and the youth in the child—we must certainly not expect the child or the youth to
act or think as if he were already a man, but
respect loyally the stage reached (*Student's
Froebel*, pp. 17, 18), the poet would again
have agreed with the educationist. His
own trouble at the crisis of his life was to
break with his past and with the great
principles of growth. He came to see that
only as each part of life is read in the light
of the whole, and is loyal to the whole, do
we live truly. He came to understand that
not only is the child, by the laws of growth,
and by the very quality of life, " father of the
man," but that only as the man is loyal to

the principles of his childhood does he reach wisdom and power.   Our theory of life, our scheme of discipline, must embrace and do justice to all parts of life, and be capable of interpreting and fulfilling its powers genially throughout its course.

Then, connected with points we have just touched, there comes up here a truth of which the *Prelude* is full.   By its temper and its theme the poem stresses, over-stresses it may be thought, the deep individuality of all real education.   It is, to some, one of the offences of the *Prelude* that it is so intensely individual.   It has been said that the " hero " in all parts of it is William Wordsworth, austerely complacent as he reviews everything in his story from that standpoint.   We have said the *Prelude* wears an aspect of that sort.   It was in the special subject and plan of the poem.   It was in the quality of the poet.   It was part of his independence, of his life-long self-reliance.   It was, besides, in the movement of revolt, and romanticism.   The return to nature was in part a return to the individual.   It affirmed the interest and worth of each man.   It stood for his " rights."   It stirred him to a sense of his place and his powers.   And in many a passage of the *Prelude* all the goings and

even the "ends" of nature appear to find
their function and centre in the child of the
Derwent Valley, in the boy of Esthwaite
Vale, and in the young man of later days.
For our serious poet it almost seems as if
the "Wisdom and Spirit of the universe"
had set and shaped all things to build up
this human soul.

And surely in a deep, and a very true
sense, it is so. In respect of education it certainly is so. As subjects of that process we
are each of us centres, and must be treated
as such. All that is done is ours only as it
comes that way, in that relation. It must
come for, it must act on and through our
minds. The idealist is right there. We must
all be individualists so far. Nature and
the scheme of life, as it goes on around us,
play on us at every moment as persons, and
the result as "read," as "organized," is personal.

This was one of the truths of "the Revolt," we have said. It seems now to some
of us perhaps a truism. No one who has
measured the significance of the truth will
think so. But in any case our educational
schemes and methods must accurately recognise it, and in so far as they do not, or
do not cordially take account of it, they

are working on wrong lines, and in a wrong spirit. Every mind must be treated as an unit, and as a moral factor, with respect for its powers and for its uses, and especially with respect for its own proper good.

There is, of course, that other truth which "the Revolt" did not see, or saw very partially, which Wordsworth saw in time, and which our recent developments in various ways have been bringing out and emphasizing, the truth without which education could not go a step—the truth that intelligence and morality are social. It is through the general mind, the "universal heart," that we know each other. It is the "common reason" that makes knowledge possible, and society. It is the will towards a common good that humanizes and unites. But the truth of "the Revolt" stands, if it must submit to a larger reading, for it is only through minds that you have mind, only through personalities that reason and conduct are possible. And so in our methods as in our ideals of education, not only at the top, but right through our system, we must loyally recognise the personal constitution of mind, and the sacred rights of every child and every youth to be and to remain a person, while at the same time we understand that paradox of the higher reason, and open secret of the true life—that it is only as each accepts the " common reason " and serves the " general good " that he reaches and fills out his true nature. The value of our results both practical and in-tellectual largely depends on our knowing how to recognise both sides of this truth and the scope of this law.

Another truth the *Prelude* finely illus-trates, and towards its close strongly in-sists on, is this—that any education that is mainly intellectual is so far forth futile and injurious. You must get, and cultivate, right, sound, active, vital feeling. In a phrase of this poet that is in true sympathy with the best naturalism of his age, the " vital soul " is the ground of all real edu-cation, and the free expansion of the " vital soul " is the true end of education. In the case of Wordsworth this doctrine, which he held strongly, and never wearied of urging, was cordially out of the poetic mind. It was also on his part, especially in the *Pre-lude*, a protest against a narrow and really absurd intellectualism in which he had him-self been caught for a time. In the crisis of his life, when the new democratic move-ments were disappointing him, and his Re-

publican hopes were in distress, when the
Revolution in France seemed a satire on
freedom and an insult to reason, the young
poet took up with the philosophy to be found
in Godwin's *Political Justice.* According to
that philosophy, if we may roughly sum
it up, our only hope lies in each man be-
coming, and the ideal state will be reached
when each of us has become, an independent and rational agent. And for Godwin,
who complacently sought to spread his
own type over the wide and various field
of human function and character, it was all
a matter of reason. When you have got
men completely rationalized, and when they
have made use of their trained reason to
adopt a sound philosophy, the problems of
education and of society too will have been
duly solved. You will then have got en-
lightened citizens in a reasonable social
order. And Wordsworth took up that
position, and held it for a time (cf. *Prelude,*
bk. xi. 224–254). But it was only for a
short time that so narrow and morally un-
genial a doctrine could have seemed to him
tenable, not to say adequate. By his build
as by his culture it could for him have been
possible only for a short time. And, in
fact, he soon saw, and felt to the very heart

of it, the narrowness and absurdity of such a philosophy. It ignored a great part of human nature, and lacked the root power, the propelling and sustaining force, of life. It left out in apparent strength, in real weakness, that which gives life its energy and interest, and very largely its meaning and its value — the " vital soul " — the life of feeling, and all the wealth and energy of the heart. In the closing books of the *Prelude* the poet dwells earnestly on this truth. And in other poems of his great period it is a leading idea. There is no real and right growth for human minds without depth and cordiality of feeling. The culture that does not give this is barren, and in a large degree a failure. Knowledge without this is almost nothing, and little good. Whatever is merely formal and not vital is a mistake; whatever tends to dull or impoverish interests to narrow or deaden feeling, is not only a loss, but an injury. The cultivation and enrichment, the direction and development of feeling, is in a sense the end and finer use of knowledge itself. To bring out and organize, to enlighten and get power for a body of just and noble feelings is a better and wiser result, and for the happiness of the individual, as for the good of society, a finer and more valuable result, than any merely or mainly intellectual culture. So this poet held with a strengthening conviction. Such, it seems to us, is the truth, a truth of first-rate importance in education.

Closely connected with the foregoing principle are other truths to be found in the *Prelude*, regarding it as a study of education. Wordsworth held very strongly, in spite of the notes of austerity and parsimony to be felt in his poetry and in his character, that a great and necessary force in the growth of mind, and in the evolution of will and character, is what he terms " vital feelings of delight." Through things kindly fitted to our natures, and to which our natures are in turn genially fitted, the mind is fed and grows. Through genial relations to all the things that are ours the spirit in us, which is right feeling and right reason harmonized and united, grows rightly. This poet held indeed, as all his readers know from certain lines of the great *Tintern Abbey* poem, that it is really through " the power of joy " that we " see into the life of things." A certain deep yet frugal pleasure is for him the medium of light, and the true pitch of life. His poetry is full of the spirit and results of this conviction. It was for Wordsworth a poetic and an ethical law. His whole view of life is full of the light of it. His view of the world is so. His simplicity, his matter-of-fact quality, in art as in life, are made beautiful by his cordial and pervading sense of this principle.

This principle has other bearings of course, since it is a principle of poetic apprehension because it is a principle of things, and on these we shall touch later. Our concern now is with its bearing on the method and spirit of education. The older educationists had made everything, or most things, hard, distasteful. They even seemed to act on the principle that the educational value of things in a course of training turned on their hardness, their unpleasantness. The early sentimentalists in education, following Jean Jacques, their prophet, went to the opposite extreme. Just as they went to the extreme of individualism, abolishing constraint and authority, they went to a kindred extreme here. They wanted to make everything easy, genial in the shallow sense, and agreeable at once. We were to slide along on the level, or the line of ascent was to be so nearly level that we

should never have the sense of effort. But
very plainly that is not the order of the
world. The conditions and circumstance
of life, however they got set, have not been
set to that strain. And to follow that strain,
that quality and method of work, were to
degrade and enfeeble humanity. Wisdom,
goodness, joy, have all another strain than
that. Happiness of the healthy and lasting,
of the permanently stimulating sort, has
ever a strain of austerity and strenuousness
in it. It comes of the play and equilibrium
of the finer forces of our natures. Our
work, therefore, and all real discipline of
mind and will, must be keyed to this, only
remembering that work and discipline are
not ends in themselves, that our end is life
and the good of life, and that the last test of
the right life and its proper activities is the
good they bring.

This matter of pleasure, when it should
arise and to whom it should come, raises
questions that are highly important in education and in conduct. The sentimentalists
—and they are " still in the land "—seem to
think that the pleasure should arise " all the
time," and that " pleasure " is the end.
The individualists hold that the pleasure
should accrue with " quick returns " to each

individual. But such positions unguardedly taken are misleading, and have, in fact, misled not a few since the gospel of Rousseau began to be preached. The truth is that in education and in conduct our aim must be set and our effort adjusted not to the nearer pleasure but to the larger good. We must learn more and more to regard the common reason as our standard and to take the common good as our law ; and the scope of all just and real education is to bring the subjects of it to this power and to this aim.

In keeping with the foregoing truths, and, in fact, as our poet thought of matters, springing out of some of them, is another, that the closing books of the *Prelude* set forth with emphasis (cf. bks. xii., xiii.)—this, viz. : that the right method in knowledge and therefore in education is constructive, not analytic ; that the real apprehension of things is a creative and not a mechanical process. Taking things to bits, and regarding them singly, we never know them. Taking them coldly, and through a medium of logical processes only, we never grasp them, and cannot give them to other minds. We must grasp them as living facts, in a whole that itself lives for us. In analytic

processes "we murder to dissect." In that
kind of approach to, and investigation of,
things the life, the reality of things, escapes
us. Merely intellectual processes of the
type of 18th century rationalism, of the
type of Hume's critical scepticism, give us
no contact with things, and certainly no
hold of them in their proper reality.

The loss of a true hold of, and vital interest
in, things was a great part of the trouble of
Wordsworth's mind at the crisis of his life
(cf. bk. xi. 270–320). Things went "meagre
and stale," all the things of human life and
of the world too. He tried to recover his
faith, his interest, in things through reason-
ing and intellectual appreciation; but this
only aggravated the trouble. His sceptical,
analytic habit, his demand that each thing
should "prove" itself at the bar of the
"abstract reason," only brought the very
"crisis of his strong disease."

What brought his cure? How did he
recover again a real hold of things and a
right relation to them? This is the " bur-
den " of the last three books of the *Prelude*.
Briefly and simply it may be said his cure
was wrought by his again taking up a true
relation to things, and by a right use of his
powers in their apprehension, since the only

cure for a malady that has arisen through thought is a deeper and truer thought. It is not easy to give more fully and still very briefly the "argument" of these books, which tell of this new method, and give the "secret of the new life" of the poet. Yet some of his phrases put clues in our hands: "genial faith," "sympathies" with and "love" towards the things of life and of nature, "wise" as poets and "as women are" (cf. bk. xii. 68–72, and ll. 156–8), truths of "the universal heart," "spiritual love" that is one with intellectual power, and imagination that is one with "reason in her most exalted mood" (cf. bk. xiv. 187–205). Keeping in view only the matter that now concerns us, since there is a good deal of other matter in those books, it will be seen that the author of this poem might have entitled his organ of knowledge Imaginative Reason. It is through processes akin to the poetic, it is through imagination as the faculty of vital constructions, the faculty that "strikes into one" and sees things from the heart of a vital appreciation—it is thus that you get at things and know them. There must be a genial care for things. There must be an intellectual love of them. We must value the fact of things without self-regards and with no vain or mean comparisons. We must bring a spirit that feels and appreciates. We must open eye and heart to their life. We must bring an active, not a passive, taste to the apprehension of them. Enjoyment more than criticism is wanted—a spiritual rather than a microscopic view. We must judge not by abstract standards, by "rules of mimic art applied to things above all art," but by intuitions of things taken in their own life and place. Our judgments of things must be not of "one sense," but of "all the senses," and of our free and total power, and our knowledge result of

> A balance, an ennobling interchange
> Of action from without and from within ;
> The excellence, pure function, and best power
> Both of the object seen and eye that sees.
> (Bk. xiii. 370–78 ; cf. 151–57.)

And again he gives his method and secret in the lines (bk. xiii. 206–7) :—

> In Nature's presence stood as now I stand,
> A *sensitive* being, a *creative* soul.

It is, then, by faithful use of this method and function of mind that we gain a knowledge of things. It is through such method and power that we can give a knowledge of things. Only the mind that has the life

and interest of things in itself, in its own
honest care for, and appreciation of, them,
can rightly teach, conveying the interest
and life of things to other minds. Only one
who stands " in the light of things," with
power over them through a degree of
imaginative reason, can give those things
to be possessions of other minds. And this
is the truer because the end of the business
of learning is not merely to have a knowledge of things, but to get the truth and
worth of things to enrich one's own life
—the " vital soul " in each of us. And if
any should stumble at the poet's phrase,
there are others in which it can very well
be put. Put it thus: Knowledge itself is
never a true end any more than the things
you can gain by its means are such an
end. It is life, and the wealth and good
of that, that are the end. And no one more
than the teacher needs to keep this wisely
and steadily in view, not as a " counsel of
perfection," but as a constant test of right
method and results in educational work.

Cognate with the point we have just
handled is a point we have already touched,
but which it will be well to deal with here,
since it runs through the *Prelude*, and is
indicated in more than one happy phrase in

the poem. We refer to that subtle conception of the nature of mind, its laws and mode of operation, which the poet owed partly to Coleridge, but mostly to his own genius as a master of the moral nature of man: the conception, namely, that mind is vital, organic, built up of living elements by organic processes, experiences, and actions, not by mechanical additions. The poet is here, again, in sympathy with Froebel, who was but little of a psychologist, and with the best psychologists of both schools since the organic conception entered the science. The finest expression of the idea in the poem is in those lines (bk. i. 340–47), but most of the poet's references to mind and to his own growth are fully in keeping with them :—

Dust as we are the immortal spirit grows
Like harmony in music ; there is a dark
Inscrutable workmanship that reconciles
Discordant elements, and makes them cling together
In one society.

The idea of mind as a living power, formed by, yet informing, all experience, is present in those lines—poetically, not psychologically, of course. Our concern with them is, that they are well on the path of the right idea, and that this idea of mind as organic in its nature and operations is an idea of fruitful importance in education. It is impossible to do more than suggest the bearings of the idea here. It seems well to do so much. The mind, then, is a living power—active, not passive. Intelligence is a vital function. It is not merely taking or reviving impressions, absorbing or arranging "facts." Knowledge is creative apprehension. Perception and memory, as well as conception and judgment, are vital constructions. The relation of states of mind to their objects may be as obscure as Professor James argues; but the mind is a living force, not a camera, and thought a function of life, not of mechanism. As organic, the mind is, moreover, a living whole. Every moment of conscious life is a vital unity, and so is the whole complex life of the mind.

But how does such conception of the working of mind apply, and what value has it in education? Some of its bearings have been usefully developed by Froebel and by Herbart. The well-known and fruitful dictum of Froebel, that only by creative activity does mind grow and knowledge become real, springs from such a conception of mind; and the kindergarten is a fruit of it. And

Herbart's idea of the operation of mind as
" apperception " is from the same principle.
The mind is built not by notions or words,
nor by things or facts, but by its own
activities and by all it becomes. You have
to deal with a living whole of actions and
reactions, and you have to work in your instruction, your knowledge, on those terms,
as a living addition to such a whole of life.
It has to find its place in such a whole. It
will live and serve only as it is fitted within
mind as such a whole. You do not " put "
knowledge into the mind, nor do you " accumulate " it within the mind. Something
called " knowledge " may indeed be " put "
there and " accumulate " considerably, and
nothing be known at all. The aim of
education is not of that sort. It is to pro-
mote and unfold those activities of mind,
that evolution of mind, through which only
knowledge is real and by which only it can
be retained and used. And this is still
true if we agree that there is no process
nor any product of mind that can be shown
to be independent of experience.

When we turn to the question of *the
factors of education*—the means and powers
by which the growth of the human soul is
promoted—it is a commonplace to say that

this poet counted nature, external nature, and the total order and beauty of the world, as one factor, and a great one. In its early books this poem is largely the record of the influence of nature on the poet's own mind. It seems to be a common opinion, among such as know Wordsworth and do not know the history of the nature senti- ment, or even English poetry before Words- worth, that he " began " this sentiment, and first " preached " education through nature. He did not begin it, but he was the first to grasp the sentiment to its depth and ex- emplify its influence and scope as an educa- tive power. And it was he who first taught us the love of nature, and a free response to her, in her whole extent. In doing this he was profoundly right, and thereby he not only enriched the poetry but the life and thought of England, and the resources of culture for ever.

There are many lovely and many strong and subtle passages in the *Prelude* in which the work and influence of nature on the mind are set forth—passages, too, in which the poet gives us a philosophy of the educa- tive influence of nature as he read it on the basis and from the vantage ground of his own experience. And those passages are not "sentimental," nor do they deal with what is called the picturesque and romantic parts or aspects of nature only, or chiefly. In early days the poet began to feel influences deeper and subtler than those of the external beauty of nature. The peace and loneliness of nature, a certain mystic depth and suggestiveness in her life, and something of her grandeur and awe began to be felt even in his schooldays. It was years before the full sentiment of nature, her vital loveliness and greatness, were appreciated; but she was pretty soon a moral influence on his mind and in his life.

And his philosophy of this influence of nature, of which the chief exposition is in the *Prelude* and in the *Tintern* poem, is interesting, and touches other points in his scheme. The poet holds that mind and nature are fitted to each other; that they act and react on each other. Our minds are not aliens and strangers in the world when we arrive here; we are fitted to our scene of life. Beauty old as creation touches us, gladdens us, because our minds and our senses have been formed by the very powers and processes that have given form to all the beauty of the world. We respond to, we interpret, nay, in our finest moments we

"create," the truth and loveliness and
splendour of the world, because the life of
our senses, and the laws of our minds, are
wrought in true affinity and vital correspondence with these. The "Spirit of the
universe," that gives to all natural "forms
and images breath and motion," builds up
our souls by pure response to "works"
that are the expression of a life akin to
our own.

It was a bold doctrine at the time when
the *Prelude* was written, and even when it
was published. It was, we may say, a hypothesis devised to account for the action of
nature on the poet's own mind, and the
extraordinary freshness and vigour of that
action. The sense of loveliness and joy that
fell on his heart at dawn, or at midnight, or
in the glory of the day, by the waters or
among the hills, when the voice of winds or
the stars of night touched the springs ot
feeling—that sense of beauty, that deep
response of the soul to the life of things,
seemed too great to have grown up in his
brief life-time, in his single life. So he
thought.

And now we should say that the poet's
intuition, or hypothesis, must, in some sense,
be true. We are made for nature, and

nature for us, to train intellect, feeling, sense, and all the passions that build up our minds in wisdom and strength. And the pity of it at present is, that so many of us have to go months and years without any real contact with it, so that many are losing sense of nature's eternal function in respect of human health and happiness. The growth of the mind and the heart cannot, in such cases, our poet held, be sound or satisfactory; and no doubt he is right. For, with some over-stress, he stood for a great truth, and for a true law of culture. Those of us who have scarcely ever seen the dawn, or felt the freshness of the morning, who have scarcely ever stood under the open sky and seen some wide landscape full of light and air, who have never felt the loneliness and peace of nature in quiet places, who have never in some still hour stood under the arch of the midnight sky alone— such, and there are not a few of them in our towns to-day, miss not only precious knowledge of the great world, but knowledge of themselves — of the heart, and the high powers of emotion and thought.

And our poet recognised almost more emphatically, though that is by no means a common opinion, our human environment and our close and healthy relation to human life as a factor in our culture. He sees and sets forth in some remarkable passages of the *Prelude* his conviction that this is a condition of all culture that is real and to the quick. It is by touch with others, by knowing others, by taking and keeping in simple fidelity our due place with other lives, our full and frank relation to them, that "the human heart by which we live" is unfolded and nourished in us. The poet is grateful that he grew up in the freedom and simplicity of the little country town of Hawkshead, scarcely more than a village. When he returns to Hawkshead and the simple home where he had lived during his schooldays, he sees its human facts from a new point of view, and feels in a new and deeper way their interest, and something of their pathos and their moral significance. His very passion for nature, his sense of her grandeur and loveliness, gave an added meaning and dignity to human life, for nature is not merely the theatre of human life, she is the minister and teacher of man. He shares her life, he reads her meaning and rejoices in her beauty. She reflects something of her glory and her amplitude on man, even on peasants as they go about

D

their tasks and live their lives in her presence and by her help.

Thus it happens that this poet of the *Prelude,* who for many is no more than the poet of nature, is also the poet of the *Excursion*; is in truth even more the poet of simple lives and virtues, of rustic men and women, and the teacher for all of us of the precious life to be won, and the mellow wisdom to be got, from the essential virtues and simple tasks and relations of every honest human life. It was part of the " malady " of his crisis—that time when the good of things, their vital ground, seemed to have gone—that he lost the simple, cordial sense of the worth of the common life. It had gone dull and small; it had come to seem "a kind of trouble of ants" on the surface of a vast mechanism we call nature Both the world and human life had lost their " soul," he says—their substance and their value. And the recovery of his humanity, and a new conviction of the spirituality, the livingness of the world, brought back to him his poetic power—gave him that power, indeed, for the first time fully. He felt as he had never felt before the pure and tender interest of human lives, and a kind of sacred beauty in the simplest.

We may smile at his *Peter Bells* and *Simon Lees*, and even at his *Margarets*, his *Pedlars* and *Leech-Gatherers*—and they are rustics of course—but the vision and truth they are the vehicle of is a vision and truth of increasing value, and one that, whether for discipline or for life, can never grow old.

The position taken in the *Prelude* on this matter, and the strong conviction of the poet that no part of culture is so important as true human relations, raises the question of the best environment for this part of training, and the place of school life in it. Wordsworth was sent to school at Hawkshead when only eight years old, and he was there until he was seventeen. But the life at Hawkshead was of the simplest and most frugal kind, and extremely natural and homely. The boys were no way a class apart. They lived in the village, and the homely village life was a part of their lives. They knew the men and women of the place, and its events, its joys and sorrows. And Wordsworth holds that such normal environment and healthy experience of life is best. The heart is nourished, and grows familiar with the quality and relations of life, its facts of good and ill, of joy and

sorrow, and in time understands and re-
sponds to them.

To many this will seem but a part of this
poet's "rusticity," and almost stoical fru-
gality of experience. Yet on the main point
we shall agree. A full and free natural
environment is better for this part of training than an artificial one, and things on this
side of life are learned rather by examples
and deeds than by words. A selected environment for the better education of youth
was one of the ideas of the poet's age.
Wordsworth prefers the natural circumstances of life, and the children trained
healthily amid such circumstances. In this
matter, too, his "love of nature" sways
him, and he prefers natural children, with
their wits and feelings in sound order, to
the children of artifice and pressure. His
scheme is home and school life, not school
life only. He would have recognised the
moral training in a good school system,
and given it a high value, but as poet and
moralist he clung to the daily humanities.
It is, of course, in part, a question of what
you are training for, and of what your
ideal of life is. If you are training for life
simply as a rough struggle of wits and
wills, and your ideal be skill and success

in such a contest, then a certain school system will give the training you want; but if your aim be a friendly and generous life and character, and a society whose citizens live in this spirit with each other, then perhaps the poet is right.

It is impossible to read the *Prelude*, especially to read it as a suggestive study of education, without thinking pretty frequently of Rousseau and the views he expounded in his *Émile*. There is little evidence that Wordsworth had studied the theories of Rousseau seriously; but the ideas and spirit of Rousseau were "in the air," and to get clearly the significance of some parts of the *Prelude*, it is useful, it is even necessary, to compare the two writers. On this matter of the scheme and factors of a true education a comparison is interesting; and on comparison important differences are found. Rousseau proposes an artificial scheme—he would isolate, and select conditions. He is thus working to a more or less abstract standard, and would form the child to a pattern of his own, while he regards himself as defending it against everything that might hinder or even disturb the natural development of its powers. And pretty largely Rousseau's " nature " and

his " natural being " are a fiction of " the
revolt." He assumes a body of " native "
instincts and impulses, which are there to
act and which know what to do. As a consequence his doctrine is to a great extent a
glorification of impulse; his scheme a plan
to give leisure and scope to individual pre-
ferences. But life is not such a sphere, nor
is society such a structure as he imagines,
and no individual is ever constituted in the
way he assumes. If the individual were
such as Rousseau assumes, and his relation
to society such as Rousseau supposes, then
one could quite understand why social relations should bring feelings of constraint,
and why it might be well to get the young
into artificial utopias to train them freely,
congenially. On the other hand, if the true
individual and society belong to each other,
and are closely interwoven from the first,
the whole situation is very different from
what Rousseau imagined, and our poet's
views represent a better philosophy and a
wiser *régime.* His is the old method of
the world, we may say. He sees in the
wholesome relations and process of life
itself a priceless education for heart and
will. For him the natural discipline and
setting of life is best. In that order, helped

by the experience and by the love of others, and stimulated by our relations with them, we learn a careful wisdom, and that love of our kind without which "we are as dust," and life a thing of little worth.

Rousseau resented "interference," and stood for "the rights of nature." Wordsworth had a vigorous part in the protest, we have seen. But in his maturity he felt another resentment, and made another protest—those against the rash theorist and the sentimental reformer. One of these protests is to be found in the *Prelude* (bk. v. 347-363), where he speaks of—

These mighty workmen of our later age,
Who, with a broad highway, have overbridged
The froward chaos of futurity,
. . . ; they who have skill
To manage books, and things, and make them act
On infant minds as surely as the sun
Deals with a flower ; the keepers of our time,
The guides and wardens of our faculties,
Sages who in their prescience would control
All accidents, and to the very road
Which they have fashioned would confine us down
Like engines ; when will their presumption learn
That in the unreasoning progress of the world
A wiser spirit is at work for us—
A better eye than theirs, most prodigal
Of blessings, and most studious of our good,
Even in what seem our most unfruitful hours ?

There is a "naturalism," modest and truthful, a moral induction, patient and very cautious, only impatient of self-confident meddlers and their ways. Now in this passage and the parts of his "argument" connected with it the poet was protesting against certain changes and on behalf of certain principles. He is opposed to those who would be for ever "instructing" and "improving," and who recognise nothing for education but their sort of instruction and improvement. He dislikes the self-conscious intellectualism and moral priggishness which their sort of education tended to produce, and holds the freedom and simplicity of his own training to have been better, and to have taught him greater things, besides giving his true nature a deeper stimulus and a sounder ethic. He draws "the model child" of the new education, "a miracle of scientific lore," shut "within the pinfold of his own conceit," and, for all his lore of science, shut away from nature (*Prelude*, v. 298–340). He wholly prefers "a race of real children; not too wise, too learned, or too good," but fresh, buoyant, natural, serious at times, and full of spirit (cf. *Prelude*, v. 411–420).

The protest here is not yet out of date on

the intellectual, or on the moral side of it. But as against this new type the poet gives certain further points in his own training which we ought to note : (1) The place of free reading from pure interest, and the worth of that. (2) The uses of romantic and childish literature. (3) The place of sports. (4) The proper spirit of youthful effort. (5) The worth and power of wonder and awe in the training of character.

Wordsworth put less value on books than most of us do, but he counted it one of the advantages of the simple scheme of education at Hawkshead that there were a few good books there, and that he was left free to read them out of pure interest in the spirit and matter of them. These books counted for much in opening his mind. They make a short list, but they are all good : Fielding, Swift, Cervantes, Lesage. They made a stronger impression on him than his class work. And it is a thing of the first importance for a capable young mind to come for itself into contact with the great minds that live through literature. The better part of education is in that contact. But what can be done to this end ? Books can be put within reach, and inducements given to read them, or else the matter be left quite open if the books be there. There is the difficulty of time and "used up" interest, which our crowded curriculum makes; and there is the danger, great at present, or reading the many books that are worth so little, and often nothing at all, and leaving unread the great books. The whole matter demands thoughtful attention.

Then it is interesting to find the poet defending against the prosaic educationists of his day the beautiful uses of the old romances and fairy books (cf. *Prelude*, v. 341–46). After naming some of them in glad reminiscence—*Old Fortunatus, Jack the Giant Killer, Robin Hood*, and " Sabra in the Forest with St. George,"—he says:

> The child whose love is here at least doth reap
> One precious gain,—that he forgets himself.

Further on in the same book of the *Prelude* (v. 460–78), he tells of a certain " yellow canvas-covered book," containing some of " the Arabian tales," which led him to long for the whole collection. The typical 18th century mind did not know the moral or the intellectual worth of these things, but it was fit that the poet of the new romantic movement should thus early respond to the charm of the old romances, and he speaks finely of their appeal to feeling and imagination — those "dreamers" and "forgers of fairy tales" who make us strangely aware of

> Faculties to whom
> Earth crouches, the elements are potter's clay,
> Space like a heaven filled up with northern lights,
> Here, nowhere, there, and everywhere at once.
> (*Prelude*, v. 510–33.)

It is a further point of interest in the *Prelude*, the zest with which this boy threw himself into the sports and pastimes of his youth; the zest, too, with which the poet describes them and the place he assigns them in the "growth of his mind." In that he is English. Thousands of youths have done and will do that. That is a lively form of "self-education," it may seem, and one we have carried pretty far, without any poet's encouragement. There are schools, it is hinted, that exist largely for that form of education. That it is education, not exercise only, and valuable education too, goes without saying. But the points to be noted in the parts of the *Prelude* in which the poet describes the sports of his youth are that they are all associated with nature, and that some of the subtlest and deepest glimpses into nature of the poet's school-

days arose in connection with those plea-
sant sports. The keen play of the senses
and the nerves, the state of exhilaration and
delight connected with healthy sports in
the face of nature, were the occasion of
those insights, doubtless. But the fact has
possibly an educational value. It points to
more than the poetic sensibility of this lad.
It points also to the extraordinary purity
and delicacy of the senses when cultivated
by vigorous exercise and constant contact
with nature. The pity of it is that our
sports are so often dissociated from nature,
and that they seem to leave no leisure for
what of nature there may be about (cf. bk.
i. 326–339, 425–498, 567–596 ; bk. ii. 5–77,
115–137, 164–175 ; bk. v. 364–388).

There is another point that comes up in
connection with these sports, but has a
much wider bearing. This poet condemns
emulation and rivalry in sports and in
studies. On both lines the competition was
" mild " in his day. We have developed it
greatly since the early years of this century.
Wordsworth was quite against it. To him
it seemed the poorest of principles to appeal
to in education, the least fruitfully stimulating, and, as a motive with reference to
character, the least social and humanly

serviceable. For himself he refused to act
on it, and indeed he acted through life on
the contrary principle, standing with stoical
independence on the merit of his work
whatever it might prove to be.

The principle of rivalry has gone deeply
into our system of education since then.
It is indeed now assumed to be a fundamental principle of the struggle of existence
and of the progress of life. It is a fair
question what our standard of "progress"
is in that case, and whether the best common good is not better. In any case we are
paying a good deal for this "competition"
and our constant appeal to this principle
of selection; and it behoves us to see what
we are doing, and whither it is taking us.

It is said that you cannot get the general
mind to work without, that you will not
get the best results of the best minds without "emulation." Our poet, on the contrary, urges that "toil and pains should
spread from heart to heart" by sympathy
and by the spirit of the place and the
society (bk. iii. 378); and that knowledge
should be "sincerely sought and prized for
its own sake" (bk. iii. 389–90). He says
elsewhere (in a letter of 1846), "I have
from my youth cultivated knowledge for

its own sake and for the good that may come out of it." It is pretty certain that he there speaks for the highest class of "workers" of every sort. Truth and beauty can only be won on terms of pure service. The more we can get of such "service" the better. And if we urge that our "great competitive system" is simply a rough and ready test for the readiest, if not the best, practical talent, let us give it the value it has in that way. Only let us make a strong stand against covering the field of educational influence and work with the spirit and appeal of emulation. For even if it be admitted that it must come into play in practical life, and that it is a part of life's discipline there, that may be a reason against, and not at all in favour of, bringing it into the earlier years. It is surely to be desired that those years should be kept for higher and more generous emotions and principles.

Then in the matter of education, conceived as a full and genial growth of mind, there is a further principle in the *Prelude* we ought not to omit, and that is the value the poet puts on the emotion of admiration deepening into wonder and awe. This is a chord of the romantic spirit which the

Prelude, like other works of its author,
frequently strikes. It was in part because
in his own experience nature, in impressive hours and great phenomena,
struck this chord so strongly, that he urges
her function in education, her value for
imagination. He thought his age lacking
in what was for him a principle rather than
a sentiment, and it was one great aim of
his art to recover and interpret this principle. Are we not in some danger of losing
it? Is nature not made often enough to
seem a great and interesting machine, and
nothing more? Is there not a tendency for
our "little light" to banish wonder and leave
only curiosity, and in certain cases a sense of
our own cleverness chiefly? But the "higher
mind" is then best nourished and expanded
when it is drawn on to admire and feel little
of itself and much of the greatness of the
world that offers itself through all experience to be known.

"We live by admiration," says our poet.
And for him the principle of wonder meant
not only that there is more to be known,
nor only that that more is immeasurable,
but that it is of such sort that it upholds and
cherishes the amplest and best life of our
minds. And then only are we "reading"

things rightly when our science has this result. There is a kind of teaching which makes knowledge and the world too seem little and of no great interest. And there is a way of teaching which makes knowledge, as a human achievement, seem great, yet hardly touches the sense of wonder at all, and never the sense of worship. Yet the latter is not more necessary to consummate knowledge than it is to stimulate mind, and only the teaching that modestly has it can reach the finer results, or maintain them through fruitful activity in the life of the mind.

And if the *Prelude* has thus our poet's intuition of the greatness of the world, it has even more distinctively his sense of the greatness, and what is often called the spirituality, of the mind. " Dust as we are " our natures have yet an " immortal " quality. Through spirit we have intuition of the nature of things. Through wisdom and goodwill we share that nature. We have seen how the poet implicitly held the organic quality of mind. We have noted his large and subtle conception of "the growth of mind," and how his idea of the correspondence of Nature and Mind carries in it a large and subtle conception of "the history of mind." And we have seen how

for our poet mind is a "creative" power,
and knowledge a "creative" interpretation.

In this he is romantic, not rationalist.
He is here in sympathy with Coleridge, in
reaction from Hartley and against Hume.
He was one of the first to strike the roots
of his view of human nature into the deep
grounds of the new thought. He is "tran-
scendentalist" as well as romantic. He was
one of the first to reject the mechanical
theory of mind—one of the first to get a
glimpse of the evolution of mind in relation
both to its own life and the life of nature.
Very largely through sympathy with the
moral nature of man, and through an
original insight into, and an independent
judgment regarding, moral facts, he got
behind the sensualism of Hobbes, the
individualism of Locke, the atomism of
Hume. For him mind is great, not merely
through its achievements, but in its principles and its essential relations. The most
living part of a living universe, it has not
only been built by the elements and laws
of that universe through its whole process,
but it stands somehow above it as inter-
preter, clothed with a power and a dignity
that are all its own. The play of nature's

forces and relations upon mind does not explain mind, nor the tissue and structure of inferences from any sensuous experience as such. Mind brings a principle of its own to give structure and meaning to such experience, and is aware of a Law above all laws—of a Reason that is the "fountain light of all our day," the "Master light of all our seeing."

But whether this be true or matter of opinion only, what has it to do with education? Not a little, as it seems to us. It is enough to suggest its bearings. The great teachers have been those who have worked with a great and fruitful idea of mind, and of human nature. A temper of exhaustless interest in, and of reverence towards, the human mind is needed if the teacher would keep the patience and gather the wisdom required for his work. Only such interest and reverence can help him to watch, or enable him to guide, that fair development of minds which is his best task and his finer reward. For if the poet's idea of the nature and destiny of minds be right, then knowledge is for minds, not minds for knowledge. Mind is greater and richer than the science we have hitherto systematised, than the art we have so far

shaped; and the temper of the true teacher,
and the scope of his teaching, will recognise this even where such recognition is
very simple or may be quite implicit. It
will be seen in his respect for growing
and flexible intelligences. It will keep him
from pedagogic hardening and dogmatism.
It will be felt in his spirit of openness and
hopefulness towards young minds. It will
lift, ahead of means and tasks alike, a
generous notion of what these minds ought
to become—a fair ideal of the life that
belongs to them, and will give, too, a
grounded hope of its realisation.

Then these later points bring us to certain ethical ideas of Wordsworth's poetry
which have such bearing on education that
we must, at least, indicate that bearing ere
we bring this paper to a close. Most of the
poet's critics have dealt with those ideas in
a wider relation. M. Legouis has an interesting criticism of some of them in the
last part of his *Study*. But there is one
that is not dealt with, and that is not perhaps easy to state fully. It is the way in
which our poet reached his sense of ethical
reality, and took up that posture of interest,
acceptance and free response to life and the
world as they are around us, which is a

critical point in the development of most
natures. This is sometimes dealt with as
" the rise of belief," sometimes as the awak-
ing of " moral consciousness." In the case
of a good many in recent years, as in the
case of Wordsworth, it may be said to pass
through more than one stage, and to be
consummated only after a " crisis." In
its main principle it is the sense of ethical
reality, the sense of a world and an order
of life about us which sets the conditions
of our lives, and towards which we must
take up a certain posture. Like most who
have lived, and learned by living, our poet
passed through a period of alienation and
even revolt, and thereafter came to a time of
cordial acceptance and loyal response. He
then knew his place, the meaning of duty,
and the worth of things, for the first time.
He not merely recognised that a man must
put himself into the world as it is because it
is his only world, but he took his place in
frank and simple allegiance and obedience
to the great order in which he found himself.

Is one mistaken in thinking that many—
that all—natures of any force and independence, of any earnestness or ideality, need
wise help here, and that the time when
such help is needed is always critical?

Goethe recognises the crisis in his *Wilhelm Meister*, and Carlyle in his *Sartor*; and Omar Khayyám, in a different temper, long before either. It comes as we become aware of will and judgment in face of a " world "; it comes acutely with the sense of a world that does not answer to desire or to reason apparently, and is thrust upon us. We then need the poet's truth. We must be brought to see that our " seed-plot of time " is our one field, and that we must take it heartily and till it, "for good and all." To unfold " belief " in this sense, to cultivate a ready allegiance to reality, is an important part of training, and if life does the greater part of it, wise help can often guide heart and will to the right attitude and decision.

This will appear a small matter, a slight achievement. It may even seem that most minds achieve it unawares. We should say that such is not the case, and that most minds pass through the " crisis " we are describing when they turn from dreams and fancies, and wishes, and vague hopes, that yet are scarcely hopes, of a scheme of life shaped to the heart's desire, to accept the fact as it is and make what they can of it. But not to get farther than this were certainly to stop at the beginning. To

accept reality, even if we accept it ethically,
with a frank determination to take it for
all it is worth, is to have got but a little
way. If we "nor love nor hate our life,"
we shall hardly, any of us, most of us
pretty certainly will not, "live well what
we live." Much reasonableness, a certain
goodness, a certain austere pleasure can be
got on those terms; but that loyalty to and
zeal for reality, without which most find it
impossible to live "well," demands more
surely. We need for that not only the eye
to see the fact, and the will to take it for
all it may be worth, but the heart to love it.
And how get and how keep that? Through
perception of its lovableness, through the
conviction that it is good. But the fact,
as it is, is not wholly fair or good, and it
often seems hard to put the heart cordially
into it. To the poet, as we have seen, it
was so at one time. All things in the life
of man seemed worse than unprofitable, and
the world itself dull and poor. Through
the "thinking heart" it was that he again
took up the facts of life and of the world and
found for the first time their simple beauty
and goodness, and a meaning in them that
proved to be now too rich for words.

It often seems as if this part of vital

culture were omitted or forgotten. It is thought, perhaps, that every one can get at this "secret" for himself, and that none can really help another. Yet one great lesson of this poetry is that a mind that has the secret can put other minds on the track of it, and even make it one of their possessions. The joy of beauty, the sense of good, a deep faith in things, and a strong, simple love of man can be thus communicated. Can any gift of culture be more precious? Yet often enough this sense of the interest and worth of life and of the world is the one thing education fails to give. It fosters a certain impatience with, or superiority to, the old and simple things of the world. It begets a tendency to pessimism. It raises a doubt whether goodness be worth the effort it costs, the reward it brings. To such cynicism and leanness of soul the poet virtually says, "Open your eyes to the world, your hearts to the life about you. Learn to see things through faith in and love of them, through their 'total beauty and meaning,' not through their 'partial appearances.' Live simply for high ends. Put yourself in touch with your kind. Learn to care for them if only because they are tied up in the same bundle of life with yourself.

Learn the value and beauty of simple lives
and lowly virtues. Set yourself to live
kindly with all sorts of men, and you will
soon find that the best you can bring to the
general good will seem all too little. And
therein you will have found that which
gives satisfaction through the sense of a
growing and an infinite good. "

Wordsworth's conviction of the goodness
of things and of the worth of life was thus
a moral intuition and an imaginative truth.
It did not rest on any dogma, and still less
on any dream. It rested squarely, we may
say, on a poetic construction of the life of
things in relation to human nature and the
mind of man. He gave up his dreams—his
scheme of a world as he would have it;
he gave up his revolt from a world that
would not have his dreams thrust on it
there and then; he gave up his rationalism, his abstract scheme of a world according to reason. And for what did he give
up dreams, doubts, and the dogmas of reason? For the customary way, for the old
tradition, and things as they are? No, not
so really. What he did really, and what
gives value, on the large question in hand,
to the *Prelude,* to the *Lyrics,* and even to the
Excursion is this, as it seems to us, that he

says on this question through the whole of his mature work, "Take the world and the life of man as they are, make the best of them, and you will find that all necessary good is possible. You will find the adequacy of the kindly honest life, however simple. You will find besides that the life and powers of man make his spiritual hopes reasonable. And you will join the great fellowship of men moving towards the unknown goal with patient and splendid trust." So we read many passages which it is impossible here to quote. And if we read them rightly you have there a temper and a truth needed then, needed now, and good always. Well is it for the youth, or the man, whose larger education brings him to these convictions, and settles him in this spirit, in despite of all that fights against them.

Butler & Tanner, The Selwood Printing Works, Frome, and London.

www.ingramcontent.com/pod-product-compliance
Lightning Source LLC
Chambersburg PA
CBHW021534270326

41930CB00008B/1243